AMERICAN REVOLUTION

A History from Beginning to End

Copyright © 2016 by Hourly History.

Table of Contents

Chapter One

A Series of Oppressions

"I am more and more convinced, of the propensity in human nature to tyrannize over their fellow men."

—Mercy Otis Warren

The late eighteenth century was a time of upheaval. Government, religion, and the concept of personal liberty were all being reevaluated through the lens of natural law, science and Enlightenment thinking. The effects of these revolutionary ideas on the far-flung British colonies in North America were to violently change the world and bring about the birth of a new nation unlike any that had come before.

The thirteen British colonies in North America were: Delaware, Pennsylvania, New Jersey, Georgia, Connecticut, Massachusetts Bay, Maryland, South Carolina, New Hampshire, Virginia, New York, North Carolina, and Rhode Island and Providence Plantations. The colonies were a business venture for the English crown, and were only a portion of the colonies Britain had founded in the New World. These colonies provided Great Britain with a rich source of goods, including cotton, tobacco, furs, fish, iron ore and lumber. Many of the colonists and their families had migrated from Great

Britain in search of religious freedom and greater opportunity than was available to them in their homeland. They remained proud of their heritage and their status as British citizens. British culture was seen as the ideal to be emulated in fashion, literature, art, and education, even though the distance meant news from England was necessarily delayed by months. The additional fact that the early colonists had had to undergo great privations, dangerous circumstances and hard work in order to build their colonies in what had been the great American wilderness, led to a population of people who were self-reliant and resentful of attempts to curtail their freedoms.

Great Britain at this time was arguably the most powerful nation in Europe, if not the world. The British Empire had been growing for two centuries and it was vast. The Empire included the American Colonies, Canada, and South America, along with rich holdings in the Caribbean. England's navy, used normally in protection of the Empire's world-wide trade routes, ruled the seas. Great Britain was a powerful ruler and protector for her colonies, and a fearsome enemy to her foes.

Beginning in 1754, American colonists were fighting the French and Indian War, which would come to be known in England and France as the Seven Years War when battle was joined in Europe two years later. The colonists were fighting the French for control of the Ohio Valley, near the Allegheny and Monongahela rivers. French troops made alliances with Native American tribes to fight against the British and Americans who were taking over ancestral tribal lands in the Ohio Valley. In 1758, British representatives were able to convince many of the tribes to support the British against the French during a meeting at Fort Bedford. This undercutting of the French alliance deprived them of a large portion of their forces, leading to the French being driven completely out of North America by 1763.

This war caused England to incur a massive debt. In order to raise the money needed to fulfill the debt, Great Britain determined that the colonists should help pay for the war via new taxes levied on the colonies. The first step in Britain's revenue raising campaign was the Stamp Act of 1765. The Stamp Act required printed materials in the colonies to use stamped paper that was produced in London and carried an embossed revenue stamp. Colonists disagreed with the stated reason for the tax, the need to keep British soldiers in the North American colonies after the French and Indian War. Colonists also felt the Stamp Act was a violation of their rights as English citizens in that the tax was levied without their consent. The slogan, "No taxation without representation," became a rallying cry for protests throughout the colonies.

Chapter Two

Death and Taxes

"It cannot be good to tax the Americans... You will lose more than you gain."

—Thomas Hutchinson

One group in particular took up the cry and the cause of resisting unfair taxation. The "Sons of Liberty" was the name taken by resistance groups causing disturbances to the collection of British taxes throughout the thirteen colonies. British tax collectors were threatened, burned in effigy, and even tarred and feathered until many of them simply retired out of fear. Groups were started in colony after colony sporadically, but they became organized around the group started in Boston.

In October of 1765, the Stamp Act Congress took place in New York City, and was the first time representatives from the colonies met as a unified group in common purpose. The congress sent a petition to Parliament and King George III that included objections to the imposed tax. The petition lined up with British merchants' complaints about lost business in America due to the protests, disturbances caused by the Sons of Liberty and product boycotts, and taken together had the effect of Parliament's repealing the Stamp Act in 1766.

Parliament was not willing to cede their right to tax British colonies, in spite of the colonists demand for representation and the failure of the Stamp Act. The Townshend Acts were passed by Britain beginning in 1767, and included the Revenue Act, the Indemnity Act, the Commissioners of Customs Act and the New York Restraining Act. These acts of Parliament were ostensibly meant to raise the money needed to pay governors and judges in the colonies. This would have the effect of keeping officials loyal to the crown paying their salaries, rather than the people they were supposedly serving. The predictable resistance among colonists to these newly imposed regulations led to British troops being stationed in Boston to provide an occupying force in the contentious city.

The occupation soon led to conflict between the red-coated British soldiers and the colonial citizens of Boston, especially since the troops were being housed by local citizenry. The most well-known of these altercations is called the Boston Massacre by the colonists and the Incident on King Street by the British. It started when a mob of Bostonians surrounded and harassed a British sentry. When more soldiers arrived to support the beleaguered soldier, the newcomers were met with by threats and a barrage of flying objects. They responded by firing into the crowd. Five Boston citizens were killed. The British soldiers were tried for murder and two of them were convicted on the lesser charge of manslaughter. The rest of the troops withdrew from the city to Castle Island, a fort on Boston Harbor. News of the events of the day spread quickly through the colonies, causing further anger to arise towards British rule. As a result of all of the unrest and protests against the new regulations, Parliament repealed all of the Townshend Act except the tax on tea.

As the tea tax remained in place, so did the colonial boycott of tea. The British East India Company, which brought in trade and revenue for Great Britain was becoming overwhelmed with unsellable tea stock rotting in its warehouses. As a move to support the East India Company and at the same time solidify the right of Parliament to tax British colonies, the Tea Act of 1773 was passed. The act gave the East India Company the right to ship tea directly to North America without passing through England first, as well as allowing duty-free export of tea from the company's London warehouse. The result of this financial manipulation was to allow the price of East India Company tea to undercut the price of black-market tea being bought and sold in the colonies as a response to the colonial boycott of taxed tea. Even with the tax on the tea, it was now less expensive to buy tea from the British East India Company. This meant that purchase of the tea also legitimized the hated tax and therefore the acceptance of Parliament's right to implement taxation. Colonists saw the implications of this plan and decided to step up boycotts of tea throughout the colonies.

When colonists demanded that ships in Boston Harbor leave and take their cargo of tea elsewhere, Royal Governor Thomas Hutchinson refused to allow the ships to leave the harbor. This left the ships unable to unload and unable to leave. The standoff continued for twenty days, which was the legal deadline by which the ship's captain was required to unload and pay the duty tax on the shipment of tea. On December sixteenth, a group of the Sons of Liberty disguised themselves as members of the Mohawk tribe and boarded the three ships waiting in the harbor. They dumped the entire cargo, three hundred and forty-two chests of tea worth nine thousand pounds, into Boston Harbor. This act of defiance has become known as the Boston Tea Party, and inspired similar actions in the other colonies. Revolutionary leader and later President of the United States John Adams wrote of the event, saying, "This Destruction of the Tea is so bold, so daring, so firm, intrepid and inflexible, and it must have so important Consequences, and so lasting, that I can't but consider it as an Epocha in History." He, along with the rest of the world, would soon find themselves embroiled in these "important consequences."

The British government saw the destruction of the tea as an act to be punished, and responded by closing the port of Boston immediately until the tea had been paid for by the colonies. Parliament passed the Coercive Acts in an effort both to punish the unruly colony of Massachusetts and bring all of the colonies back in line. Thomas Gage was appointed Governor of the Massachusetts colony, effectively overriding Massachusetts' right to self-government in favor of a more immediate role for British rule. The colony was also limited to only one town meeting per year. The Administration of Justice Act meant that the British Governor could order trials for public officials to be held outside of Massachusetts if he felt a fair trial would not be held in the colony. This meant that witnesses would have to travel to the new location at their own expense, making it financially impossible for most colonists to testify. George Washington called this portion of the new legislation "the Murder Act," because he believed it allowed British officials to escape justice for crimes committed in the colonies. The Coercive Act also included a legal right for the governor to take over buildings in order to house British troops.

The colonists did not respond well to these actions of Parliament, and came to refer to them as the "Intolerable Acts." Citizens in Massachusetts who had not taken part in the Boston Tea Party felt they were being unfairly punished for the actions of a few. Citizens in other colonies were concerned by the enforced reorganization of the government in the Massachusetts colony, and feared it could happen just as easily to them. Instead of settling the revolutionary state of the colonies, the Coercive Acts had the effect of solidifying the distrust and dissatisfaction with British rule.

Chapter Three

Out of Many, One

"I am not a Virginian, I am an American."

—Patrick Henry

As a result of the growing unrest, the thirteen disparate colonies began to join together, with England as the common enemy. Most citizens were not as yet convinced of the need to separate from England, but the actions seen as tyrannical rule were universally resented. To cement the unified resistance, the First Continental Congress was held in September 1774 at Carpenters' Hall in Philadelphia, Pennsylvania. Several men who would come to play a key role in the American Revolution attended this first meeting, including George Washington, John Adams, Samuel Adams, Patrick Henry, and John Jay. The Congress resulted in boycotts of all British trade, as well as an appeal sent to King George requesting the repeal of the Coercive Acts. They also decided they would meet again the following year if the appeal did not have the desired effect of halting the enforcement of the acts. In the meantime, the representatives determined that the colonies should be raising militias in preparation for repercussions from England.

In response to the increasing militarization in Boston and the surrounding area, the British government declared Massachusetts as a colony in rebellion in February of 1775. British troops were ordered to capture and destroy stockpiles of military supplies rumored to be held by rebels in Concord. The colonists became aware of the secret orders issued to British troops and prepared to defend their armory. In Boston, when local patriots became aware that the British troops were on the move and were planning an attack by traveling the Charles River, they set in motion the plan to notify militia groups in the nearby towns to prepare. Famously, two lanterns were hung in the tower of Boston's Old North Church to notify watchers on the other side of the river of the British movements. Also, patriots Paul Revere and William Dawes raced toward Lexington and Concord on horseback to carry the warning and raise troops along the way. Church bells rang out, drums beat throughout the night, and more riders took off in other directions, carrying the news to the country-side. Paul Revere made it to Lexington by midnight where he was able to warn Sam Adams and John Hancock.

When the British troops advanced on Lexington on the morning of April nineteenth, they were met by colonial militia forces. It is unknown how the battle began, but the first shots of the war were fired at sunrise in Lexington. After the initial skirmish, the outnumbered colonial militia fell back and British troops continued on to Concord and split into companies in their search for military supplies. Colonial militia fighters took advantage of the smaller numbers of the British search groups and attacked a group of about four hundred soldiers at Concord's North Bridge. Even though the militiamen outnumbered the British troops they were engaging, both sides suffered casualties before the British forces retreated to join the rest of the forces in Concord. As the entire force of British troops marched back toward Boston, more militia members joined in along the route and harassed the British line all the way to Charlestown. The events of this day were memorialized by Ralph Waldo Emerson in his poem, "Concord Hymn," in which he described the initial gunfire in this skirmish as "the shot heard 'round the world."

As the letter sent by the First Continental Congress in 1774 was seen to have no effect, the Second Continental Congress was held on May tenth of 1775. The congress was held in Philadelphia, Pennsylvania one month after the events at Lexington and Concord. This second meeting of representatives included members from all thirteen colonies and also brought in two men who would play memorable roles in the years to come: Thomas Jefferson and Benjamin Franklin.

The Second Continental Congress started out facing a war, based on the fighting that had already occurred. In June, the group voted to establish a Continental Army. The army was at first made up of the militia groups already in existence around Boston and commanded by General George Washington, the representative from Virginia. The congress created two seemingly contradictory documents, the Declaration of the Causes and Necessity of Taking Up Arms, and the Olive Branch Petition. The declaration, as its name suggests, spelled out the reasons the colonists found it necessary to take up arms against Great Britain, including what they felt to be violations of their rights as British citizens and reiteration of the efforts that had been made to address the issues peacefully. The petition was a final attempt by the members of the congress to reconcile with the British government. It reiterated the loyalty of the colonists to Great Britain, and pleaded with the king to address the issues enumerated in the letter sent by the First Continental Congress.

Chapter Four

War in Earnest

"Don't fire unless fired upon, but if they mean to have a war, let it begin here."

—Captain John Parker

During this time, the colonists in Massachusetts became aware of British troop action meant to set up positions on the hills surrounding Boston, effectively cutting off the city. So, with little time to prepare, and with its commander still involved in the activities of the congress, the newly formed Continental Army began constructing its own fortifications on Breed Hill. The original battle plan had called for the use of nearby Bunker Hill, but the army, under Colonel William Prescott, settled on the closer hill. The ensuing action would be forever known as the Battle of Bunker Hill.

On June seventeenth, 1775, Major General William Howe led British troops from their landing on the Charlestown Peninsula toward the waiting colonials on Breed's Hill. Colonel Prescott is famously supposed to have ordered his men not to fire on the approaching British soldiers until they could see the whites of their eyes. This command may have been a strategy to conserve ammunition, but it may also have been a reflection of the inaccuracy of many of the militia's weapons.

The initial British attack was repulsed by the punishing fire from the colonial guns; however, they quickly recovered and struck again. The outnumbered colonial militia men were forced to retreat and the British won the day, in spite of the large numbers of casualties the Americans had been able to inflict. It is estimated that the British forces suffered a thousand dead or wounded while the Continental Army bore one hundred dead and three hundred wounded. Even though the battle resulted in British control of Boston, the colonials were encouraged by the amount of damage they had been able to inflict. This battle was the first real indication that the newly formed army stood a chance against the might of professional British soldiers.

It was after the battle of Bunker Hill that General George Washington joined the soldiers already making up the Continental Army in Cambridge Massachusetts. There he found a disparate group of volunteer riflemen with inadequate weapons and supplies. While some of the wealthier militia groups had uniforms and consistent weapons, most of the soldiers wore simply their normal civilian clothing and carried their personal rifles. Even when the colonial government attempted to outfit the troops, it was difficult because of the lack of manufacturers for the needed supplies.

The majority of the men that made up the army had very little experience in soldiering other than whatever they had learned as a militiaman. Many were young men leaving home for the first time, some as young as sixteen years old. Discipline and cohesion were nonexistent in his new command, and he was faced with the daunting challenge of preparing to fight the most powerful, professional and well supplied army of Europe.

In October of 1775, Parliament officially declared war on the American Colonies. During this time, the Continental Congress in Philadelphia decides to ban black soldiers, whether slave or free, from serving in the Continental Army because Southern slave owners were against arming black Americans. Britain took advantage of this stand taken by the colonists to issue a proclamation freeing any slaves or indentured servants, regardless of color, who join the British army. This resulted in a rash of slaves rushing to support the British cause against the already outnumbered Americans.

Great Britain responded quickly and in force. The British navy, then the greatest naval force in the world, sailed for New York. General George Washington prepared for battle.

Chapter Five

Voices of Liberty

"There is something very absurd in supposing a continent to be perpetually governed by an island."

—Thomas Paine

The popularization of the teachings of the Enlightenment movement raised a new desire for personal freedom, as well as disillusionment with the idea of the divine foundations of monarchical rule. New ideas were coming to the forefront of public consciousness, and adherents to these ideas engaged wholeheartedly in speech and in print with the goals of revolution.

One famous American who spoke publicly in the cause of freedom and revolution was Patrick Henry. Politician, planter, and lawyer from Virginia, Henry gained recognition for his oratory prior to the Revolution. His efforts to raise opposition to the hated British Stamp Act led to his most famous speech, which gave rise to the impassioned phrase, "Give me liberty or give me death!" His words were used as a rallying cry for revolutionaries fighting for independence from Great Britain.

In the opening days of 1776, a new voice joined the revolutionary cause. Thomas Paine was a recent immigrant to the United States from Great Britain. He wrote a pamphlet entitled "Common Sense," which was published in Philadelphia on January tenth and immediately became a best-seller. "Common Sense" was a stirring call to revolution, based on many of the same ideas as Enlightenment works popular in Europe, but expressed in the language of a Protestant sermon, which all of the colonists were very familiar with.

Paine used "Common Sense" to detail various forms of government throughout history, and discuss the purpose of government in society. He laid out examples of the failures of monarchy as a system of government as part of his argument for independence from Britain. He put forth a plan for a governmental structure for the colonies that would be completely new, as befitted a nation that would be founded on independence and natural rights. Paine's suggestions very closely resemble the government that was eventually adopted by the new United States of America.

Thomas Paine would continue his writing career with great success over the course of the American Revolution. Although "Common Sense" was his most popular and influential work, many of his later works would also chart the course of the growing American discontent and then the war. "The American Crisis" was also published in 1776, and its tone of encouragement in the face of desperate odds illustrated the sweeping changes that had taken place once the exhortations of "Common Sense" had been enacted by the Colonials. General George Washington had the pamphlet read aloud to his troops in an attempt to raise morale with Paine's fiery rhetoric.

Chapter Six

Independence

"My hand trembles, but my heart does not."

—Stephen Hopkins, Rhode Island delegate

In July of 1776, the Continental Congress decides to declare the thirteen colonies independent from Great Britain. Representative Thomas Jefferson is chosen to write a formal Declaration of Independence to explain the rationale behind the vote to separate from Great Britain. Thomas Jefferson's first draft is edited and finally ratified by the Congress as a whole on July fourth. The declaration was widely distributed throughout the colonies in order that all citizens of the newly christened "United States of America" might read the rationale behind their revolution.

The opening line of the Declaration of Independence states, "We hold these truths to be self-evident, that all men are created equal, that they are endowed by their Creator with certain unalienable Rights, that among these are Life, Liberty and the pursuit of Happiness." This one line from the Preamble is ground-breaking and provocative in and of itself. The idea that a high moral truth could be proven and upheld simply because it was commonly evident, without the intervention of some higher authority, would have widely been considered blasphemous mere decades before. The audacious claim is that all men should be equal was in direct opposition to the cherished Western tradition of the divine right of kings to rule, as representatives of God's will on Earth. It was a direct rejection of the British monarchical government as unnatural and unjustly founded. Further, the claim that the common man did have rights granted by their Creator apart from laws of man was revolutionary.

The assertion of unalienable rights enshrined in the founding document of the United States is controversial from the start in a nation where slavery was legal and upheld. Slaves across the colonies understood the contradiction between the high principles in the statement and the reality of their daily lives. Hundreds took this as an announcement of their own right to freedom and escaped from slavery. Slaves owned by Thomas Jefferson and even George Washington escaped, starkly underlining the hypocrisy written into the nation's consciousness.

After the powerful Preamble, the Declaration goes on to detail a list of oppressions that King George had unjustly visited upon the American colonies. The list of oppressions included: the king's failure to assent to laws passed by the colonial government, and even to ignore pressing legislation altogether; the dissolution of representative bodies that allowed the people to take part in legislation; the creation of new governmental offices with their accompanying "swarms of Officers"; the maintenance of military forced in the colonies during times of peace; depriving colonial citizens of fair trials while setting up "mock trials" for members of the military who stood accused of crimes; the issuance of taxes without representation; and the dispatch of more military troops "to compleat the works of death, desolation and tyranny, already begun with circumstances of Cruelty & perfidy scarcely paralleled in the most barbarous ages, and totally unworthy the Head of a civilized nation." In summary, British rule was depriving the colonists of the freedoms they felt were theirs by natural right, and they were therefore justified in declaring independence from that rule.

The signed document was sent to the British Parliament. This was a point of no return for the colonists. The men who signed the declaration were now criminals in the eyes of the British government. Benjamin Franklin addressed the group saying, "Gentlemen, we must now hang together or we shall surely all hang separately."

Chapter Seven

New York

"Let us convince every invader of our freedom."

—Samuel Adams

New York City, at the time of the Revolutionary War, was of course not the iconic metropolis that it is today, but by virtue of location it was already a strategic jewel in the conflict between the colonists and the British. Situated on the coast and with the mighty Hudson River as a portal to the interior of the continent, the city was an obvious port city with an impressive natural harbor. Controlling New York City meant control of the eastern seaboard. Founded by the Dutch as a trading center and originally called New Amsterdam, it was captured by English forces in 1664 and renamed New York City in honor of the Duke of York. The city was the setting for many of the fiercest battles of the war, and American prisoners of war were held throughout the war on British battleships anchored in the harbor.

The British attack on New York under General Howe continued unceasingly and forced American troops out of New York by September. In a rout, colonial lines broke and soldiers fled away from the city. Over a thousand of the colonial troops were left behind as British prisoners.

Rather than taking on the remnants of the scattered army, the British forces hold and allow the Colonial army the chance to escape and continue the battle.

Colonial troops retreated north along Manhattan in disgrace. The leadership of George Washington fell under question and many members of the army deserted. The British army was left in control of New York City and the Hudson River. It was a crushing defeat for the Continental Army.

In an attempt to regain momentum in the war, General Washington planned an audacious attack on Britain's paid Hessian mercenaries. Knowing that the Hessians would celebrate the Christmas holiday and be unprepared for battle, Washington arranged an attack on the British stronghold in Trenton, New Jersey. Forces of the Continental Army crossed the partially frozen Delaware River in shifts on the night of December twenty-fifth, using whatever crafts they could find along the shore. Once across, they stealthily surrounded the British position and readied themselves to attack.

The attack resulted in an overwhelming victory for the Continental Army. The Hessians, who had indeed been celebrating with copious amounts of alcohol, were completely unprepared. Men stumbled, partially dressed, to confront the attackers, but were soon subdued and surrendered the post. The colonists captured more than a thousand prisoners, along with their stores of muskets, powder and artillery. The victory bolstered Washington's position as the military leader of the Continental Army and also improved the morale of the soldiers who had seen defeat throughout the preceding year.

Fighting continued the following year, most notably at Fort Ticonderoga on Lake Champlain. The Fort had been of great strategic value during the recent French and Indian War, and had ended as a British possession. In the current action, the strategic value was not seen as important as it had been previously due to the location of the combatants. The British troops manning the fort had been lulled into a false sense of security by their years of service in what was then a wilderness outpost. They were unprepared for attack, and the fort had been captured by the Americans in 1775 in a joint action led by Colonel Benedict Arnold and Ethan Allen's Green Mountain Boys, allowing for much needed stores of weapons and ammunition to fall into American hands. Ethan Allen took full credit for the capture of the fort, not even mentioning Arnold in his report to Washington. This slight is considered as part of Arnold's motivation in plotting to betray the Americans toward the end of the war once he was in command of West Point.

In July of 1777, however, Fort Ticonderoga was retaken by the British force under Lieutenant General John Burgoyne. When the commander of the occupying forces of the Continental Army, General Arthur St. Clair, saw that Burgoyne had the fort surrounded and his army seriously outmanned, he ordered his troops to withdraw and escape. Although there was some gunfire, and a few casualties, the British force was able to occupy the fort with very little effort, though they would not hold it for long.

After several months of fighting with few victories to show for it, including the uncontested loss of Fort Ticonderoga in July, the fortunes of the Continental Army were about to change for the better. Having been forced into a strategy of slow retreat, the Continental Army spent some time encamped near Stillwater, New York. Aware that British forces under General Howe and General Burgoyne were moving south towards the location of the colonial camp, General Washington ordered reinforcements from nearby militia to join the army at Stillwater. Under the command of General Gates, the Continental Army moved north, towards the oncoming British. They set up fortifications on the defensible Bemis Heights near Saratoga, where the terrain created a funnel through which British troops would have to pass. The two armies faced off on September 19th, 1777.

Action began when advanced scouting parties led by Daniel Morgan's men, largely frontiersmen skilled in woodlands combat, and the light infantry troops commanded by Henry Dearborn came in contact with an advance company of General James Hamilton's forces. Initially attacking the British force by use of marksmen sniping from locations in the surrounding forest, Morgan's men were able to quickly eliminate most of the officers in the opposing company. The hardy frontier riflemen lived up to their reputation on this day. They accounted for close to six hundred British casualties in the battle. They followed the initial deadly barrage with a charge, and were able to drive back the advanced force. In the confusion, the main body of the British army opened fire on the force coming toward them, killing several of their retreating comrades.

The American victory did not stand for long, however. The full complement of the British Army under Burgoyne fought back, leading to a day of intense fighting interrupted by breaks in the action and retreats by one side or the other. By the end of the day, the British army held the field, while the Continental Army was content to withdraw and wait.

General Burgoyne received word the following day that desperately needed reinforcements under Henry Clinton would arrive in ten days. With his forces weakened and outnumbered, dwindling supplies, and food rationing already in place, the forces facing him seemed too formidable to face. He decided to wait to push his attack until Clinton arrived. Daily clashes between scouts and pickets of the two armies took place, but full engagement was avoided. The American sharpshooters harassed British troops almost continuously, picking off their targets with deadly accuracy while remaining unseen in the trees. British soldiers deserted, unwilling to continue with the army's desperate plight and the constant threat of sniper attacks.

When September slipped into October with no sign of the hoped for reinforcements, General Burgoyne's force was in a desperate situation. Several officers suggested retreat, but Burgoyne insisted that retreat would be disgraceful. The army engaged in another attack on the

American position, outnumbered and undersupplied. The British attack was quickly defeated, leaving General Burgoyne to retreat with his surviving soldiers, now outnumbered three to one by the Continental Army that drove them off. The British army under General Burgoyne was forced to surrender on the seventeenth of October. General Burgoyne returned to England, and never commanded an army again.

The Battle of Saratoga was a much-needed victory for the Continental Army. For the first time, the British were convinced that the Americans were a respectable foe, with the ability to fight a successful war. Also impressed by the American victory, the French chose finally to openly enter the war in support of the rebellious American colonies and declared war on Great Britain. When French allies including Spain and the Netherlands joined the American cause, the revolution became a world war.

Chapter Eight

Valley Forge

"We began a contest for liberty ill provided with the means for the war, relying on our patriotism to supply the deficiency. We expected to encounter many wants and distressed' we must bear the present evils and fortitude."

—George Washington

With winter setting in after a year of hard-fought campaigns in 1777, the Continental Army set up winter quarters in Valley Forge, Pennsylvania. At this point, the army was so under-supplied that only a third of the men had shoes to wear as they marched, leaving bloody footprints in the snow. Many soldiers died of exposure as they didn't have adequate clothing, and the shelters in the camp were overcrowded and took time to set up. The army lived on cakes made from flour and water, with small amounts of meat as it could be obtained. Many of the army's horses died from starvation or exposure. The close quarters and privations led to epidemics of typhoid, dysentery, and smallpox. This was a hard winter that taxed the morale as well as the supplies of the rebel army. By the time spring finally arrived, over two thousand soldiers had died of exposure and illness.

In January of 1778, five members of the Continental Congress came to review the situation at Valley Forge in response to General Washington's repeated requests for food and other supplies. After seeing the pitiable condition of the troops, the representatives went back to Congress and worked in favor of providing more support for the army. By February, Congress had approved needed funds for supplying the army, as well as organized the commissary department to maintain supply lines going forward.

In spite of the terrible conditions and the shortages of basic necessities, the winter at Valley Forge is seen in hind-sight as a turning point in the Revolution. The arrival of Baron Friedrich Wilhelm von Steuben from France with a letter of introduction from Benjamin Franklin was a much-needed boost to the effectiveness and the morale of the army. General Washington immediately named him Acting Inspector General in charge of developing a training program for the troops. A long-time veteran of the Prussian army, Baron von Steuben was an ideal candidate to train the troops. Although he spoke very little English, he carried out training and drills in a mixture of German and French, assisted by a translator. He also wrote a training manual for the troops that could be used to provide uniform and consistent instruction throughout the colonial army. A staff of translators worked tirelessly to prepare his work for use. This new manual, "Regulations for the Order and Discipline of the Troops of the United States," would be used as the official training guide for American military forces until the War of 1812.

Throughout the winter the troops drilled every day, learning how to move in orderly fashion between formations. They trained on how to accurately and quickly load, aim and fire their rifles. They learned how to effectively mount a bayonet charge. Baron von Steuben worked directly with the troops, giving commands and instructions from dusk until dawn. In the spring of 1778, the newly organized Continental Army held a grand parade to celebrate the official French entrance into the war against Great Britain. They displayed the new orderly maneuvers and discipline learned over the hard winter, showing themselves to have become a unified fighting force ready to continue the struggle for Independence.

Chapter Nine

France

"Insurrection is the most sacred of rights and the most indispensable of duties."

—Marquis de Lafayette

France had been a clandestine ally of the American revolutionaries since the beginning of the war by secretly sending supplies, but in June of 1778 France officially recognized America as an independent nation and declared war on Great Britain. Spain and the Netherlands followed France's lead, also declaring support for the Americans, leaving Great Britain standing alone against an alliance of European powers and the Continental Army.

The French were largely motivated to join the fight because of the long-standing animosity between France and Great Britain, including the recent loss of territories as a result of the French and Indian War. Benjamin Franklin, noted American writer and inventor, was the American minister to France between 1776 and 1783. He played an important role in convincing the French to send supplies and to eventually declare support for the colonies in the war.

Not the least of France's contributions to the American cause was in the volunteer service of Frenchman Marie Joseph Paul Yves Roch Gilbert Du Motier, better known as the Marquis de Lafayette. Lafayette was a French nobleman who came to the aid of the newly formed United States in 1777, joining the Continental Army at their winter quarters in Valley Forge. He was made a major general in the Continental Army under General George Washington. Lafayette proved his worth in his initial action, the Battle of Brandywine on September 11th of 1777. Lafayette was shot during this battle and still managed to organize a retreat of American forces. He soon became a close friend of General Washington's and remained a staunch ally throughout his life. He not only served as a successful commander in battle, but also used his considerable reputation in his home country to help garner more aid for the Americans from Europe. Lafayette would command multiple battles in the years to come, including the Battle of Barren Hill in which Lafayette was able to evade an attack by General Howe. Lafayette was instrumental in convincing the French to join in the war on the side of the Americans.

In the fall of 1781, the French navy and the American Continental Army tightened the noose around the British forces. The French navy, including the whole of France's Caribbean fleet under Francois Joseph Paul, the comte de Grasse, defeated the powerful British navy sailing under Rear Admiral Sir Thomas Graves in the Battle of Chesapeake Bay. This gave France command of the sea lanes around Virginia, and allowed for reinforcing of the French and American troops under Lafayette. When Nathaniel Green, American commander of the Continental Army in the south, forced General Cornwallis and the majority of the British Army to the Yorktown Peninsula in Virginia, the blockade by the French navy kept the British from escaping by sea, and also prevented any hope of reinforcements arriving. This cooperative effort by ground forces and naval assets became known as the Siege of Yorktown.

Chapter Ten

Surrender

"Yet let's be content, and the times lament, you see the world turn'd upside down."

—British marching tune

The British force was effectively penned in, with the Continental Army and French ground forces on one side and an angry ocean afloat with French battleships on the other. The French and Colonial troops set up and began bombarding the British position. Two attack groups were sent to engage the remaining British defenses. French troops overran one emplacement, while a division of the Continental Army took over the other. American artillery was able to take up a closer and more commanding position in order to continue the bombardment of the British holding. French gunmen fired upon the British fleet trapped in the harbor and were able to set fire to several of the ships. General Cornwallis ordered a desperate escape attempt. Troops were to be ferried across the York River to Gloucester Point, where they might have some hope of breaking through American lines and escape to the fortified city of New York. The first group made the crossing safely, but then the weather seemed to conspire with the besieging forces. A storm swept in, making the already dangerous river crossing an impossibility. The first group of soldiers was cut off from the rest of the army and also trapped behind enemy lines.

On October 14th, General Cornwallis sent a messenger to the Continental troops requesting terms for surrender. Two days of negotiations between the opposing forces followed, to take place at the Moore House. Negotiations were conducted between representatives of all of the forces involved. Lieutenant Colonel Thomas Dundas and Major Alexander Ross represented the British, while Lieutenant Colonel Laurens stood for the Americans, and the Marquis de Noailles for the French. French and American representatives would share equally in all aspects of the negotiation and surrender, as a reiteration of the alliance that had made the victory possible. The official ceremony of the surrender took place on October 19th, 1781.

With the entire complement of the Continental Army on one side of the road and the French forces lining the other, the defeated British contingent numbering over seven thousand soldiers marched toward the American commander to give their surrender. General Washington had denied General Cornwallis's request that the army be allowed the traditional Honors of War, which meant they would march out with dignity, their flags yet waving, with shouldered arms and with the band playing an American marching tune, because the general had denied this honor to the troops under Benjamin Lincoln when the British had taken Charleston. Instead, the surrendering army would march to the tune of "The World Turned Upside

Down" with their flags bundled and their weapons reversed in shame. General Cornwallis, commander of the British forces in North America, did not attend the ceremony, claiming illness. Instead, the General's second General O'Hara was given the task. Upon approach, General O'Hara at first attempted to offer his sword to Lieutenant General the Comte de Rochambeau, whose troops were arrayed behind him in full French military regalia. Rochambeau directed O'Hara to General Washington, who, in turn, indicated that the surrender would be accepted by his second in command, Major General Benjamin Lincoln. Lincoln marched the British troops to an open field adjoining, where they were ordered to ground their arms. Many of the defeated soldiers flung their weapons into the ground with force, attempting to destroy them before turning them over to American hands. Many soldiers are also said to have wept as they threw down their gear.

The surrender of General Cornwallis and his army meant the loss of over eight thousand British troops, artillery and horses, along with several warships and their crews. When the British fleet that had been dispatched to rescue the army arrived, they were informed by British loyalists of the surrender. General Washington sent a messenger to Philadelphia to inform the Continental Congress of the victory, and the entire town celebrated for days. It is said, when Lord North, British Prime Minister, was informed of the defeat, he responded by saying, "Oh, God, it's all over." Although King George was set to continue fighting, Parliament prevailed and Great Britain was forced to come to terms with the upstart colonies.

Chapter Eleven

An Independent Nation

"Objects of the most stupendous magnitude, and measure in which the lives and liberties of millions yet unborn are intimately interested, are now before us."

—John Adams

In the spring of 1782, talks began in Paris, France, between delegates of the United States and Great Britain with the purpose of negotiating peace. The United States was represented by Benjamin Franklin, John Jay, John Adams, and Henry Laurens. Unfortunately, the ship that was transporting Henry Laurens was captured by a British battle ship. He was imprisoned in the Tower of London until after the treaty was signed. Representing Great Britain were David Hartley and Richard Oswald. These talks would continue for the next year.

Many points of common concern were discussed, including issues of fishing rights off the North American coast, trading regulations, and debt collection, but the key point to be agreed upon was Great Britain's recognition of the United States as an independent nation. The territories previously claimed by Great Britain between the Allegheny Mountains and the Mississippi River were given over to the control of the new nation, effectively multiplying the area of the thirteen colonies ten-fold. The United States agreed to return property confiscated during the war to British Loyalists.

At the same time, Great Britain was engaged in negotiations with the other nations who had allied with the Americans during the war: France, Spain, and the Netherlands. The group of treaties was signed by the representatives of the affected nations on September third, 1783 at the Hotel du York in Paris. The document signed by the United States and Great Britain that gave the United States Independence was called the Treaty of Paris. The separate treaties with all the nations together as a whole were called the Peace of Paris.

France did not gain much in the treaties of the Peace of Paris. The expense of supporting the American cause had been great, and negatively affected an already strained French treasury. The economic situation would be an instigating factor in the French Revolution which would follow a few years afterwards.

Chapter Twelve

Constitution

"We have it in our power to begin the world over again."

—Thomas Paine

In May of 1787, representatives from twelve of the thirteen former colonies, now states, gathered in Philadelphia with the intent to amend the Articles of Confederation passed by the second Continental Congress into a federal constitution that would be the basis for government of the new nation. With this goal in mind, the group became known as the Congress of the Confederation. It was soon clear that while many of the ideas embodied in the Articles of Confederation would remain influential, the assembled group would be creating an entirely new document in creating the constitution.

The meetings of the Congress of the Confederation were held in Independence Hall, the same location that had been used by the writers of the Declaration of Independence. The building would be the scene of furious debates over the next four months as these representatives sought to forge a government that could unite the interests of the different states and represent the wishes of the people it governed. Issues such as equal representation for all states or representation based on state population brought arguments between small states and large ones. The controversial issue of slavery caused explosive debate between slave holding states and those represented by abolitionists. The importance of limiting the power of government was vital, considering the treatment the colonies had endured under British monarchical rule. Finding a solution that would work for all concerned was the beginning of a new structure for government.

The controversy between the states regarding representation in government was resolved by the creation of two powerful governing bodies; the Senate and the House of Representatives. The Senate would represent all states equally, with two Senators per state. The House of Representatives would represent the states with numbers of representatives based on state populations. Both would have power in the legislative process.

The issue of slavery was deemed too controversial to be solved by the Congress of the Confederation. Compromises were made to allow the constitution to move forward, but the issue remained unresolved. The compromise here was that the power to regulate the slave trade would move from the purview of the states to the central government after twenty years. In this way, the current situation was retained, but a forced reevaluation was stipulated for the future.

The necessity for limitation of power was met by the establishment of a multi-branch government with checks and balances built in to maintain the power of the government in separate hands. The first three articles of the Constitution detail the separation of powers. Three branches, the Executive, Judicial, and Legislative, would work together to govern the people while preventing the unequal rise to power of any one branch. Articles Four, Five, and Six describe the rights and responsibilities of state governments, especially in relation to the federal government. The new government would also reallocate power to the states, creating a power sharing model unlike anything existing at the time.

The formation of the Executive Branch was a special case. For colonists who had fought to be free from the rule of a king, a powerful executive was a controversial idea, but monarchy was the most familiar form of government at the time. Arguments were made for a single executive officer and also for a three-person counsel such as that used in ancient Rome. In the end, the vote carried a single President to head the new nation.

The Constitution was designed to be amended as the need arose. The representatives at the Congress of the Confederation hoped that they were designing a living document that would adapt to future unforeseen circumstances without losing the main governmental structure. The Constitution has been amended twenty-seven times since its passage, and remains the guiding force in the government of the United States today.

After four months of deliberation and debate, the final text of the Constitution was prepared. On September seventeenth, 1787, thirty-nine delegates signed the document, which was then submitted to the states for ratification. Article Seven of the Constitution details the procedure that would be used by the thirteen states to ratify the document. Several of the states were opposed to the Constitution, and submitted amendments to it as an addendum to approval. Ten amendments were approved by Congress simultaneously during the first session, which became known as the Bill of Rights. The Bill of Rights included: freedom of religion and freedom of speech and press, the right to keep and bear arms, provisions for the quartering of troops, freedom from unlawful search and seizure of property, the right to due process of law including the proscription against double jeopardy and seizure of property under eminent domain, the right to a speedy trial by an impartial jury with the ability to confront accusers aided by counsel, the guarantee of jury trials for federal civil cases, freedom from cruel and unusual punishment and excessive fines, the assurance that the rights specifically listed in the Constitution are not the exhaustive listing of the rights held by the people, confirmation that rights not delegated to the United States in the Constitution will be reserved to the states and, or, the people. The Bill of Rights served to allay many of the fears and concerns raised by the states, and soon led to ratification of the entire Constitution of the United States of America.

Chapter Thirteen

The President

"Example, whether it be good or bad, has a powerful influence."

—George Washington

The final step in setting up the new government of the United States was the installation of the executive officer, to be known as the President of the United States. The first presidential election was held in 1789, and former general of the Continental Army George Washington was elected. Washington's popularity and proven devotion to the cause of the revolution led to his receiving a vote from every elector in the Electoral College. To this day, he is the only president in American history to be unanimously elected. John Adams, representative of Massachusetts, himself a future president, was the first Vice President elected to the government of the United States.

As the first president, George Washington set the tone and traditions of the office that continue to be upheld. Although many in Congress suggested titles for the office that mimicked the pomp observed in European courts, such as "His Majesty the President," "His Exalted Highness," "His Elective Highness," and even "Most Illustrious and Excellent President," George Washington felt that the country had had enough of titles and insisted upon simply, "Mr. President." Washington also avoided any of the trappings associated with royalty that he could easily have assumed. He wore no crown or other "royal dress," instead wearing the clothing he would have worn as a wealthy businessman.

George Washington served two terms as president, during which time he took steps to secure the future of the new nation. Policies intended to resolve the national debt and build a strong financial footing were enacted. Treaties with Native American tribes as well as European powers gave the nation a foundation emphasizing peaceful relations. He approved the bill that established a permanent location for the nation's capital by forming the District of Columbia so that the capital would not belong to any one state, but to all. The newly established capitol was named for President George Washington. Washington helped establish the layout of the city, including the location of the Capitol Building and the White House. Although he oversaw construction of the White House, he never took up residence there.

After his second term in office, Washington faced pressure to continue his service as President. Knowing that his term in office would serve to set a precedent for future government he retired from public office, establishing the standard of the presidential two term limit that has only been set aside once in the history of the United States. Washington returned to Mount Vernon, his Virginia estate, to live out his life as the gentleman farmer he had always considered himself. When George

Washington passed away at the age of sixty-seven from a sudden illness on December fourteenth, 1799, the news spread quickly through the country. The nation mourned the loss of a great national hero, and even the British fleet paid tribute to his memory while the French observed an official ten-day mourning period.

Washington served his country as a soldier, as a military leader, a congressional representative, a contributor to the Declaration of Independence and the Constitution of the United States, and as the first President. He also served, unofficially, as an example of what the leader of a free nation should be. He was offered the chance to rule as a king, but chose instead to serve as a citizen.

Conclusion

"Whatever may be the judgment pronounced on the competency of the architects of the Constitution, or whatever may be the destiny of the edifice prepared by them, I feel it a duty to express my profound and solemn conviction . . . that there never was an assembly of men, charged with a great and arduous trust, who were more pure in their motives, or more exclusively or anxiously devoted to the object committed to them."

—James Madison

The United States of America, a nation born out of bloody battle and a fierce desire for independence, has grown from its humble beginnings to become a leading power in the world. Moving forward on the foundation set by the men who fought for freedom in the American Revolution and created a new form of government, the United States has often struggled to live up to the lofty ideals of its founding.

Eighty-seven years after the signing of the Declaration of Independence, the thirteenth president of the United States Abraham Lincoln gave a speech honoring the soldiers who fought in another battle on American soil. He described America as a nation "conceived in liberty, and dedicated to the proposition that all men are created equal." These qualities instilled by the revolutionaries remained a powerful aspect of American identity so many years later. Ironically, the battlefield at Gettysburg, Pennsylvania which Lincoln dedicated with his address was part of a devastating civil war rooted to some extent in the failure to address the conflicting beliefs of equality and the legality of enslaving men and women based upon the color of their skin.

Although one result of the American Civil War was to outlaw slavery in the United States, the issues arising from the selective nature of the equality presented as a natural right of humanity in the American Declaration of Independence have haunted the nation throughout its history even to the present day. In 1866, the Civil Rights Act gave native born Americans citizenship, but not the right to vote. It is ninety-three years after the signing of the Declaration of Independence before the Fifteenth Amendment to the Constitution, passed in 1869, granted black men the right to vote. It was not until 1920 that the Nineteenth Amendment was passed, guaranteeing the right of American women to vote. Racial and gender-based inequality as a matter of law, and the philosophical ramifications of the delay in correcting it, remain a divisive force in American culture in spite of great strides towards the cherished ideal woven into the country's identity. In spite of the concerns involving equality though its history, the United States of America has been a champion of freedom and human rights around the world. The nation's military and naval forces, which seemed so insignificant when taking on the might of the

British Empire in 1775, have become a preeminent force in world affairs.

The original thirteen colonies have evolved to form a nation of fifty united states covering a swathe between the Atlantic and Pacific Coasts, Alaska and Hawaii. The vision of the men who wrote the Constitution was a society based on individual liberty and natural rights, safeguarded by laws to prevent tyranny and ruled by the people for the people. Though their efforts did not result in a perfect government and mistakes were made that have impacted the nation for centuries, they created an entirely new form of government based on the will of the people. History thus far seems to show their faith was well founded, and the United States of America remains "the land of the free and the home of the brave."